D1608915

This Book Belongs To:

Dedicated to McKinley Goolsby...
& all the girls like me in the world.

Change the world,
You were meant for it!

Aa
is for
Ava
DuVernay

The first girl like me to make a
100 million dollar movie.

Bb

is for

Beverly

Bond

A girl like me who DJ's and created the Black Girls Rock! awards show.

Bb

Cc
is for
Misty
Copeland

The first girl like me to be principal
dancer with the
American Ballet Theatre.

Cc

Dd
is for
Brehanna
Daniels

The first girl like me to be a NASCAR pit crew member.

Dd

Ee
is for
Epsy
Campbell

The first girl like me to be Vice President in Costa Rica and all the Americas.

Ee

Ff
is for
Diandra
Forrest

The first girl like me to have albinism and be the face of a major beauty brand.

Ff

Gg

is for

Carol

Gist

The first girl like me to win the Miss USA title.

Gg

Hh
is for
Carla
Hayden

li

is for

Issa

Rae

The first girl like me to create and star in a premium cable series.

Jj
is for
Stephanie
Johnson

The first girl like me to be a
Delta Airlines Pilot.

Jj

Kk
is for
Kheris
Rogers

The youngest girl like me to debut
a fashion line at
New York Fashion Week.

Kk

Ll
is for

Loretta

Lynch

The first girl like me to be
U.S. Attorney General.

Mm
is for
Ibtihaj
Muhammad

The first girl like me to wear a hijab while competing in the Olympics for the United States.

Nn
is for
Nadja
West

The first girl like me to be a lieutenant general in the army.

Oo
is for
Michelle
Obama

The first girl like me to be First Lady of the United States.

Pp
is for
Violet
Palmer

The first girl like me to referee a regular-season NBA game.

Pp

Qq

is for

Quvenzhané Wallis

The youngest girl like me to be nominated for the Best Actress Academy Award.

Rr

is for

Rosemary
Cloud

The first girl like me to be a
Fire Chief in the United States.

Rr

Ss

is for

Simone

Biles

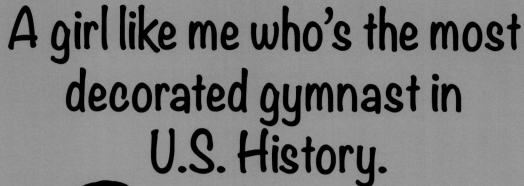

A girl like me who's the most decorated gymnast in U.S. History.

Ss

Tt

is for

Tyra Banks

The first girl like me to land the cover of GQ and Sport's Illustrated's swimsuit edition.

Uu
is for
Ursula
Burns

The first girl like me to head a Fortune 500 company.

Vv

is for

Valerie Amos

he first girl like me to head a university in the United Kingdom.

Vv

Ww
is for
Serena
Williams

A girl like me who holds the record for the most Grand Slam singles titles in the Open Era.

Ww

Xx

is for

Allyson Felix

The most decorated girl like me in U.S. Track & Field.

Xx

FELIX

Yy
is for
Yara
Shahidi

A girl like me who started an organization dedicated to bringing change to America -all while attending high school, getting accepted into college and starring in a TV show.

Yy

Zz

is for

Zakiya

Randall

The first & youngest girl like me to win First Place in the Ladies Professional Golf Association U.S. Women's Open

Zz

Now you know your ABC's & 26 Girls Like You and ME!